Humanism

Barbara Smoker

D1635838

Ward Lock Educational

ISBN 0 7062 3146 5

First published 1973
Reprinted 1976
Reprinted 1978

Set in 11 on 12 point Press Roman on an IBM 72 Composer
for Ward Lock Educational Company Limited
116 Baker Street, London W1M 2BB
A member of the Pentos Group

Printed in Great Britain by David Green (Printers) Ltd
Kettering, Northamptonshire

Contents

Preface

The word 'humanism' has more than one meaning. In its broadest sense, it is an attitude of mind that is centred on mankind and human interests. Generally, it implies a desire to think for yourself; to 'do your own thing'; to accept the results of free inquiry, whatever they may be; and to act in accordance with those results, in the light of reason, and in cooperation with others, for the promotion of human happiness.

When applied to the revival of classical learning at the Renaissance (roughly, 1300-1550 AD), the word 'humanism' stands for a passion for scholarship and the arts and a broadening of cultural horizons; but the Renaissance 'humanists' were still Christian. (Indeed, one of the best known of them, Thomas More, was canonized as a Roman Catholic martyr.) So they were not humanists in the sense in which the word is used in this book.

In our own century the word 'humanism' became a synonym for 'freethought', implying a rejection of religious beliefs based on alleged revelation. (No god; no future life.) At least, that was what was almost universally understood by 'humanism' until the 1960s. Then the meaning began to be extended to include Christians and other believers who, while believing in supernatural life, were also very concerned with human welfare in this life. This has blurred the meaning of the word, so that some humanists now feel it necessary to call themselves 'secular humanist' or 'scientific humanist', in contrast to 'Christian humanist' or 'religious humanist'.

In this book the word 'humanism' means secular, scientific humanism - that is, a positive man-centred philosophy of life based on rationalism that is either atheist or agnostic, being concerned with life in this world, not with supposed gods or a hereafter.

Probably most people in the country today live their day-to-day lives on humanistic lines, making their decisions according to experience and commonsense; but those who also follow horoscopes or superstitions, or who say prayers or believe in a future life, cannot be humanists.

The names of the philosophers and their philosophies are given in this book, not because it is necessary to remember them, but in case you want to find out more about them.

1 The humanist tradition — its beginnings

Almost every child ever born into the world must have wondered, at some time or other, how the world started—if it *did* ever start. And how they themselves came to be in it—and how they came to *be* at all.

In the beginning . . .
Learning that your parents conceived you only pushes the question back to how life began in the *first* place. Biologists are excitedly discovering the mechanics of it, but the fact that it actually happened at all is as amazing as ever. And the beginning of consciousness is more amazing still. (Without our highly developed consciousness we should not know we existed, or be able to wonder about it like this.)

People naturally like to have answers to their questions, so they have been thinking of possible explanations for existence, ever since they began to be human. The most satisfying of the explanations are handed down from parent to child, and what begins as guesswork is passed on as fact. In this way, each tribal community gradually builds up a whole body of myth to account for the world in which they find themselves.

One such explanation, constructed in Babylon about 2,500 years ago, forms the first chapter of *Genesis*. It was such a satisfying story that it spread from country to country; and even today, with all the scientific knowledge we have regarding animal evolution, and our solar system, and the vast universe beyond, some people still accept it as literally true.

Another basic thing that people wonder about is death. Life is so important to us that when we discover that all living things eventually die we want to be assured that it won't really happen to *us* nor to those we love. We are told (according to the religious tradition in which we are brought up) that we will go on living after death, through reincarnation, or through absorption into a 'world-soul', or through personal survival in another world. But is it *true*? (This will be considered in chapter 3.)

There are always some people who, though living honourable and considerate lives, are sceptical about the faith into which they happened to be born—people who prefer to keep 'an open mind' about

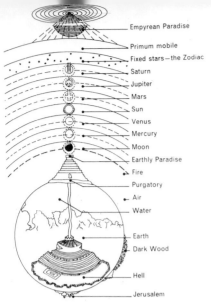

Empyrean Paradise
Primum mobile
Fixed stars—the Zodiac
Saturn
Jupiter
Mars
Sun
Venus
Mercury
Moon
Earthly Paradise
Fire
Purgatory
Air
Water
Earth
Dark Wood
Hell
Jerusalem

Dante's medieval Christian idea of the
the universe, derived mainly from
the Bible, with the after-life
abodes geographically located
(1300 AD)

the currently accepted explanations for which they see no evidence, or only evidence that is unconvincing. These people are in 'the humanist tradition'.

At some periods of history, humanism (under various names) has flourished as a respectable alternative to the prevailing creed; but whenever the religious authorities have been powerful and vengeful, those who questioned the orthodox creed have been punished and even put to death, so humanist ideas have had to go underground. But some sort of humanism has always been there, even if only in people's secret thoughts, as an alternative to religious faith.

Is it a religion?

Can humanism be called a religion, then? And, if not, what is this book on humanism doing in a series of books on different religions?

Well, it depends on what you mean by 'religion'. If you mean systems of supernatural belief and worship, then humanism is not a religion. but if you mean a philosophy that people live by, then it is. Some humanists like to call humanism a religion, while others do not. For instance, a famous humanist biologist, Sir Julian Huxley, wrote a book on humanism and called it *Religion Without Revelation,* while another well-known humanist, Mrs Margaret Knight, called her book on humanism *Morals Without Religion;* so they were obviously using the word 'religion' in different senses. I myself dislike calling humanism a religion, because it is confusing to do so. But a series of books on world religions would be incomplete without one on humanism, since it is the permanent alternative to them all.

6

The ancient Greeks

The philosophical ideas in modern humanism have their source in the thinking of some of the Greek philosophers, mainly congregating in the city of Athens, under its wise ruler Pericles, in the fifth century before Christ. Athenian culture and democracy, which liberated the individual from the bonds of clan and family, have made Periclean Athens the model for what is called 'the open society' (which is a humanist ideal) to the present day; while its rival city, Sparta, represents 'the closed society' (the totalitarian regime).

In the previous century, two great atheistic philosophers had lived and taught in the Far East—Confucius in China, and Buddha in India. For 2,500 years their ideas have had a tremendous influence, and not only in their own countries, though the systems named after them have not always kept to their atheistic origins. However, for the chief philosophical influences in the western world, moulding all its important religions and philosophies, we must look to the philosophers of Periclean Athens.

One of the earliest of these philosophers, and one of the most important to humanist thinking, is Protagoras (484?-414? BC) who founded the school of professional travelling teachers known as 'Sophists', on the principle that a little ordinary practical human knowledge is more useful than searching for the whole truth.

Protagoras taught that justice is a matter of agreed rules, not divine ordinance, and that 'man is the measure of all things'. In other words, that for human beings there is no standard, or ideal, outside human purposes and values derived from human experience and sensibility. This principle is central to modern humanism, and is in fact the main difference between humanism and religious faith. The religionist generally believes that human values derive from absolute values, originating in a god that is independent of mankind, beyond time and

Pottery picture showing Sophists in an Athenian school of the fifth century BC, giving their pupils the individual attention that helped make it an age of intellectual brilliance

beyond this world. To the humanist, this is nonsense. And so thought Protagoras, some 2,400 years ago.

Although there were humanistic ideas around in ancient Egypt, as long before Protagoras as he was before us, Protagoras is sometimes called 'the first humanist'. None of his writings (except a few odd sentences) have come down to us, but he is supposed to have written a book that began 'Of the gods I cannot say whether they exist or not'. This was probably a cautious way of saying he did not believe in them at all (for it was just as dangerous to profess atheism in those pagan times as it was in Christendom two thousand years later). Even so, there is a legend that he was forced to flee from Athens on an accusation of blasphemy.

Democritus, Socrates, Plato

Then there was Democritus. Perhaps he was a friend of Protagoras, as they came from the same city, Abdera. Democritus was a 'materialist' or 'monist'—that is, a philosopher who says that the universe is made up of matter (material things and their movements)—mind being a material process (a process of the material brain), not something different, and time and space being ways of measuring matter. Instead of starting from the prevailing supernatural beliefs, Democritus studied nature at first hand. He worked out an atomic theory (first suggested by Leucippus of Miletus) that came remarkably close to the science of our own time—saying that matter comprised changeable combinations of atoms that had always existed, the world being formed out of a primeval whirling motion. Democritus, who lived to be a very old man, was known as 'the laughing philosopher', because he used to laugh at the follies of mankind.

Also living at that time was Hippocrates, 'the father of medicine'. He and his pupils freed their minds of religion—which not only provides answers without evidence but may even consider illness to be a part of the divine will. Hippocrates relied strictly on exact observations of symptoms—and some of his medical cases are described so accurately that doctors today are able to diagnose the diseases. This scientific care was matched by the humanitarian care that Hippocrates and his followers gave to their patients, whom they took fully into their confidence; and it added up to a humanistic view of medicine that has remained the ideal for doctors to this day.

Another very great philosopher living at the same time was Socrates (469-399 BC). He wasn't good-looking, but the power and wit of his conversation could hold an audience spellbound. He used a method of

8

Sculptured head of Socrates
(469-399 BC), from whom all
the great schools of philosophy
claim descent

discussion (called 'Socratic', though probably got from Protagoras)
which pursued the truth by question and answer, 'wherever the
argument might lead'—thus fulfilling the humanist requirement of free
inquiry. Socrates said that the only way in which he was wiser than
other men was that they thought they knew a lot whereas he knew how
ignorant he was!

Socrates always insisted on terms being defined. That is to say,
'Before we start arguing, let us decide exactly what it is we are talking
about.' In order to live good lives, he said, we must be clear about what
goodness is. And he was never afraid to speak out for justice, even in
unpopular causes.

As he grew old, Socrates had a big following among the young sons
of the nobility. But, not surprisingly, quite a few people
disliked him—especially the pompous ones whom he had made look
foolish in argument. Besides, he was regarded as a threat to the
established order. So he was accused of denying the gods of Athens and
of corrupting the young. A jury of Athenian citizens found him guilty
and sentenced him to death by a drink of hemlock. He could have saved
himself by formally recanting his irreverent views, but he preferred to
take the poison and die.

There is a graphic description of his death in a book written by one
of his pupils, Plato (427?–347 BC). In fact, most of what we know
about Socrates (and, for that matter, several of the other philosophers
of the day) is from Plato's *Dialogues,* for Socrates himself never wrote
anything. He just liked talking. Plato wrote down a lot of the things he
remembered Socrates saying, and, because the educationists of later
centuries favoured Plato, his works have survived.

Plato had a religious turn of mind, believing strongly in an ultimate reality behind the world we experience. This is the theory of 'Forms' (or 'Universals'), which he took over from Socrates and built up into a whole system of thought. These Forms are ideal prototypes—'absolutes', eternal and unchanging. They exist, said Plato, in some higher world, apart from their particular manifestations which we experience in the ordinary world, the manifestations being illusion, not reality. According to this Platonic philosophy, the human values of beauty, truth, and goodness come to us from the higher world.

This is a far cry from the down-to-earth theories of Protagoras and Democritus, and comes much closer to the Christian concepts of heaven (Plato's higher world of Forms), God (Plato's Form of the Good), and the immortal soul (Plato's Form of a person) than to humanist ideas. So Plato is an *opponent* of the humanist tradition.

Aristotle

Just as Plato had been a pupil of Socrates, so Plato himself had a famous pupil—Aristotle (384-322 BC). In his hands, the Platonic Forms became 'immanent' (that is, existent *within* the natural objects) instead of being 'transcendent' (*beyond* the natural objects). Thus, instead of the ideal Form of an oak-tree existing on some other plane of reality, the Form is carried within the acorn itself, as a *potential* oak.

Aristotle had a great many interests, including language (which he regarded as a reflection of reality), ethics (which is the study of moral principles), the laws of logic, problems of causation, and the classification of plants and animals. He constructed a 'scale of nature' which was still regarded as authoritative in the Middle Ages.

Aristotle maintained that everything is caused. But to complete the chain of causality he decided that there must have been a first

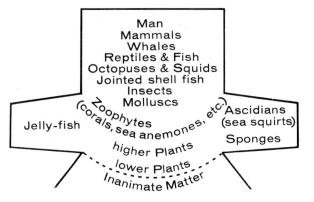

Aristotle's 'scale of nature'— showing the progression between classes of living things, up to and including man

'uncaused cause' and 'prime mover', to set the whole works going, for he found this easier to accept than the atomists' theory that matter had no beginning. He apparently failed to see that in supposing an uncaused cause he was contradicting his initial assumption that *everything* is caused! Although he only meant it as a philosophical idea, not as a personal god, the Christian theologians of the Middle Ages seized on this Aristotelian theory as demonstrating the existence of God. They ignored the fact that Aristotle had also explicitly rejected the idea that mind or spirit could exist apart from matter, thus ruling out a personal god (or angels or ghosts) without a body.

Aristotle's teaching is called 'peripatetic' (Greek for 'walking about') because of his habit of strolling round the garden with his pupils while he taught them. His three greatest achievements, to a humanist, were: his inclusion in natural science of the study of man (mind as well as body), making human welfare the criterion of moral conduct, and affirming the great potential of humanity if freed from fear of the gods. But these important aspects of Aristotle's work were cast aside by the medieval Scholastics, because they did not fit in with Christian doctrine, and they were ignored until modern times.

While Plato had used methods of reasoning to try to understand the divine scheme of things, Aristotle used the same methods of reasoning to understand how things really were, and to put them to human use. These two different ways of using reason were the beginning of the cultural division between religion and science in Europe.

Epicurus
A year or so before Aristotle died, a remarkable young student, Epicurus (341-270 BC), came to Athens from Samos. Unlike Aristotle, he accepted the atomists' theory that matter is made of everlasting atoms, so he did not need any 'uncaused cause'; and he explained the

Epicurus (341-270 BC), a materialist philosopher who found everything explicable without supernatural causes, and taught that the purpose of life is pleasure

formation of the world by supposing chance collisions that set off later events, so he did not need any 'prime mover'. He held that there are millions of worlds (what we now call galaxies) and that the gods lived in the empty spaces between them, taking no interest in men's lives, so men need not bother about the gods. And he taught a similar detachment towards life itself. He probably only brought the gods into it at all in order to avoid trouble: all that we know of his philosophy suggests that in fact he was an atheistic materialist.

A person's soul (or Form) was, he said, held together by the body, so the soul must die when the body dies. Death is simply the end of life, after which nothing can be experienced, and it is therefore unreasonable to be afraid of death. (One might reasonably fear a painful death, but that can usually be avoided by suicide.) A philosophical epitaph (in both senses of 'philosophical') appeared on the graves of many Epicureans (the followers of Epicurus) throughout Italy, Gaul, and Roman Africa: *I was not—I have been—I am not—I do not mind.*

What concerned Epicurus was the art of living. Taking as his starting-point Aristotle's principle that good conduct is that which promotes human happiness, Epicurus went on to define the good life as a life of pleasure and friendship, absence of pain, and peace of mind. His disciples included women and slaves, and all were treated as equals—an unheard-of thing! It is a common mistake (deliberately fostered by some religious people) to picture Epicureans as greedily indulging in pleasures of the body. Epicurus himself lived a frugal life, providing for his guests some cakes and water, with a little wine and cheese at festivals. And he taught that peace of mind requires 'moderation in all things'. So much for St Augustine's smear that Epicurean materialism was 'a philosophy of swine'.

The chief rival ethical system to Epicureanism in the Hellenistic and Roman empires was that of the Stoics, who believed that men should not aim at pleasure, even in the moderate Epicurean way, but should try to make themselves independent of the pleasures of life. Although modern humanists are basically Epicurean, they approve of Stoic acceptance in a bad situation when nothing can be done to make it better, but not otherwise.

Epicurus is said to have written as many as three hundred books, but only fragments have survived. Here is one of his delightful sayings that have come down to us: *Friendship goes dancing round the world proclaiming to us all to awake to the praises of a happy life.* That is humanism, in a nutshell.

2   The humanist tradition — its continuation

During the six hundred years following the break-up of the Roman empire there was so little education in Christian Europe that this period is known as the Dark Ages. Then, from the end of the tenth century AD there was a gradual revival of learning, mainly through Muslim Spain—for the Muslims had preserved some of the teaching of the ancient Greeks.

The thirteenth-century Christian 'Scholastics' set out to reconcile theology with philosophy. They believed that Christian doctrine could not possibly be against reason, and should be supported by reason. So they brought the Greek classics back into education. Little did they realize what a gamble this was.

The Renaissance
The revival of learning was very slow until, in the late fourteenth century, it blossomed into what is called the 'Renaissance' (meaning 'rebirth'). This was the transition period between the rigid formality of the Middle Ages and the enlightened freedom of modern times. The Renaissance 'humanists' (notably Erasmus and More) were not complete humanists in our sense, because they were still Christian. And the great artists of the Renaissance (like Leonardo and Michelangelo) still used religious subjects for their paintings and sculptures—but religious subjects with a very human look.

Later on, because love of the arts was thus associated with the word 'humanism', people who cared about art and literature to the exclusion of science began to call themselves 'humanists', though people in the true humanist tradition have always cared a great deal about science too. Indeed, the 'scientific method' (that is, the method of observation and experiment) is the humanist way of getting knowledge, as opposed to alleged religious revelation.

The scientific method
When scientists want to know whether they have guessed right about anything they do not look to sacred writings—they look carefully and honestly at the observable data to see whether these support or

disprove the guess. And if they disagree among themselves, they can discuss the evidence rationally, each side being willing to be proved mistaken by the other.

This scientific method is the humanist way of finding out the way things are. Like scientists, humanists must be willing to change their ideas when these do not square with what actually happens. Followers of the various religions are much slower to change their ideas, for they generally believe that God has given them the truth and that everyone else is therefore at least partly wrong. Not all scientists are humanists—but perhaps they ought to be, if people were always consistent, for science and humanism never accept conclusions as final, while it is characteristic of religion to do so.

The great historical breakthrough for science was when the new 'inductive' method of reasoning came into use at the end of the sixteenth century. ('Inductive' means forming general laws from particular instances that keep to a repetitive pattern and look as though they will go on like that for ever; it is contrasted with the 'deductive' way of reasoning from general assumptions to particular instances.) Of course, induction was not really new: it had been the method of Democritus and Hippocrates two thousand years earlier. But after being lost for so long it was excitingly new again, and it enabled men like Francis Bacon, Copernicus, and Galileo, to lay the foundations of modern natural science.

The Measurers—a painting by Hendrik van Balen (1560-1632), showing people engaged in different kinds of measurement, with appropriate instruments, to symbolize the scientific method

14

The Enlightenment

The philosophers of this modern science (beginning with Locke, and including Berkeley and Hume) were called 'Empiricists', from the Greek word for 'experience'. All knowledge of reality, they said, comes from observational experience. Empiricism was a very important step towards modern humanism, though most of the seventeenth-century Empiricists were still Christian. Those of them who denied Christian beliefs (such as John Toland) were persecuted and their books were burnt. But at that point in European history it was still confidently expected, as a matter of faith, that natural science would be able to confound atheism for ever.

Soon, however, it became clear that this confidence was unjustified, for, instead of supporting Christian doctrines, natural science came out more and more against them. A non-Christian philosophical movement called 'the Enlightenment' started in Paris with the great writer Voltaire and the encyclopedist Diderot. They and their followers are known by the French name 'the *philosophes*'. This movement spread throughout Europe, and beyond. The Churches tried to stem the tide of disbelief, but in vain.

These eighteenth-century sceptics did not go so far as to call themselves 'atheists'. For one thing, it would have been dangerous to do so; for another, science had not progressed enough yet to make it seem likely that there was no God of any kind. Most of them called

Voltaire (1694-1778) who, with his fellow *philosophes*, attacked orthodox religion and advocated social reform

MONS.ᴿ DE VOLTAIRE.

15

themselves 'Deists', meaning believers in an unknown (probably finite and impersonal) supreme being. Other names they used were 'Naturalists', 'Rationalists', and 'Freethinkers'. (The last two labels are still used by humanists today.) But Christians usually called them 'sceptics' or 'infidels'.

The most outstanding of the English Deists was Thomas Paine (1737-1809), a self-educated man who wrote three very important little books: *Commonsense,* which helped bring about the American War of Independence; *Rights of Man,* a defence of the French Revolution; and *Age of Reason* (written partly in a French jail when he was imprisoned for protesting about the unnecessary violence after the Revolution was won), a devastating critique of the Bible. 'It is the duty of man,' he said, 'to obtain all the knowledge he can and make the best use of it.'

The nineteenth century
One question that has exercised philosophers from the beginning is the question 'Why be good?' Religious people answer this by saying that man has to obey the wishes of a higher being. For humanists, though, there is no higher being to obey. So why should humanists be 'good'? This question will be considered in chapters 4 and 5; but here, in their historical place, the nineteenth-century Utilitarians must be mentioned.

The return of unbelief in the eighteenth century, with no God to be obeyed, made the question of morality an important one. It was answered, at the beginning of the nineteenth century, by the philosophy of 'Utilitarianism', put forward by Jeremy Bentham and James Mill and developed by Mill's son, John Stuart Mill, Herbert Spencer, Leslie Stephen, and others. The Utilitarians said that moral law is based upon utility—that is, upon the practical consequences of particular actions. And these consequences are to be judged in terms of human happiness. This was really a return to Epicurus, but the return had to be made in modern philosophy before humanism could be accepted as a moral system of thought.

In the middle of the nineteenth century, the English naturalist Charles Darwin, who devoted his life to the work of patient fact-finding, collected a great deal of evidence pointing to biological evolution (that is, the theory that animals slowly change from one kind to another)through a process which he called 'natural selection' or 'survival of the fittest'. This theory of evolution, which Darwin expounded in his book *Origin of Species* (1859), was strongly denounced by the Churches as heresy, for Christian doctrine taught that the different species of animals, culminating in man, had each

16

A cartoon of 1872, ridiculing Charles Darwin's book *Descent of Man*, by depicting the author as a monkey

come about by separate creation, as described in *Genesis.*

Four years later, another great scientist, Thomas Henry Huxley (grandfather of Sir Julian Huxley and Aldous Huxley) applied the principle of evolution to mankind. Charles Darwin then developed this theory in *Descent of Man,* published in 1871.

This made the clergymen and theologians more angry than ever. But exploration and research and the invention of better scientific instruments gradually produced more and more evidence for evolution, till most of the Church people gave in—at least to the extent of accepting a compromise theory, 'creation by evolution'. However, though a wonderful process, evolution hardly seems to square with belief in a compassionate creator, for it operates through the weak always going under.

Meanwhile, several new words for labelling people in the humanist tradition had come into use. In 1840 a courageous, self-educated freethinker, G.J. Holyoake, coined the words 'Secularism' and 'Secularist' (from a French word meaning 'worldly'), and these words are still used today. Secularists say that religion ought not to interfere with the law, education, and other ordinary worldly matters. In 1860, the word 'humanist' was used in print in our sense for the first time. Then, in 1869, the evolutionist T.H. Huxley coined the word 'Agnostic' (from the Greek for 'not knowing'). Some humanists still call themselves agnostic (nowadays we are more sparing with capital letters), in preference to atheist (Greek for 'without God')—though there is not much practical difference between saying that knowledge about any gods is impossible (agnosticism) and that one simply does not have any such knowledge and will therefore not assume that gods exist (atheism).

Today the more militant humanists tend to call themselves atheists, freethinkers. or secularists; while those who are more ready to cooperate with religious people and to avoid the subject of God in case it upsets them tend to call themselves agnostics or humanists—but there is no hard and fast rule about it. Other names for humanists are 'rationalist' (from the Latin for 'reason'—reason, not revelation, being adopted as the basis of knowledge) and 'ethicist' (from the word 'ethical', relating to moral questions—the Ethical Movement being concerned to establish natural grounds of morality); but these two names have rather gone out of use in Britain since the second world war.

The twentieth century
In the first half of this century there were many outstanding humanists in science and public life, but the greatest of all was an English earl, who was a mathematician, a philosopher, a social reformer, and a political rebel. His name was Bertrand Russell. Not only did he bring together many of the philosophical ideas of the past and make them more realistic; not only did he add his own important contributions to mathematics and logic; he also involved himself in education, in liberal politics, and in international affairs—for he did not think philosophers should cut themselves off from the practical issues of their day. What, he asked, would be the use of all his mathematical and philosophical work if the world were to be blown to bits in a nuclear war? So, although he was a very old man, and might well have allowed himself to ease up, he travelled to conferences around the world, continued his writing, launched the Campaign for Nuclear Disarmament (in 1958) and the Committee of 100 (in 1960), and took part in antiwar demonstrations in the streets. Thousands of young people rallied to his banner. It was like the story of Socrates over again—except that hemlock was fortunately now out of fashion. In his ninetieth year Russell was jailed, for the second time in his life, because, like Socrates, he was 'corrupting the young' and shaking 'the establishment', and he refused to promise to give up 'civil disobedience'. And from the age of sixteen, way back in 1888, he had been an atheist, a

18

The humanist philosopher Bertrand Russell (1872-1970). addressing an antiwar rally in Trafalgar Square in 1962

rationalist, a freethinker, a secularist, a humanist. He was also a strange personal link with the Utilitarians, for his godfather was John Stuart Mill!

Between the two world wars, the British humanist movement had declined in membership, mainly due to apathy resulting from the decline of religion itself. But the Ethical Union was gradually built up again after the second world war, largely through the work of its Secretary, H.J. Blackham, who later became the first Secretary of the International Humanist and Ethical Union, which he helped to found in 1952, and the first Director of the British Humanist Association.

The British humanist movement was also given a big boost in 1955 by the hysterically hostile reaction of some sections of the public and press when the BBC allowed the humanist viewpoint to be put, very moderately, by an Aberdeen lecturer in educational psychology, Mrs Margaret Knight, in a series of three radio broadcasts for parents. The extent and fury of the outcry seem almost unbelievable today. (Margaret Knight relates the story in her book *Morals Without Religion.*)

Meanwhile, science had been making huge strides, explaining more and more about the natural world and so leaving less and less for supernatural explanations to get away with.

One of the most important biological discoveries of all time was made in England in 1953 by two young men, James Watson and Francis Crick. What they discovered was the structure of the DNA molecule, which enables hereditary characteristics to be passed on from parents to offspring.

As a development from that, a French biologist, Jacques Monod, made an exciting contribution to humanist philosophy with his book *Chance and Necessity,* published in France in 1970. (The English translation appeared in America in 1971 and in Britain in 1972.) Monod points out that, as can be seen under powerful miscroscopes, the heredity of living organisms depends on chance—that is, on haphazard, unpredictable events that could not possibly have any design or purpose behind them. So everything that has ever lived, including the human species and each individual person, is an accident, started by *chance* and perpetuated by the *necessity* of chemical reactions.

This means that there is really nothing left for a creator God to do. It also means that for every person, and every living thing, there were untold billions that might have been but never made it. Don't you feel overwhelmed at the colossal odds against your having come to life at all? The last of an infinite number of chance factors that gave you life was which of millions of spermatozoa happened to reach and fertilise which waiting egg. That meeting was what created the unique person, you. It is as though you won a huge dividend in a colossal lottery that had been accumulating for hundreds of millions of years.

Monod's evidence of chance happenings upset not only theists, clutching at a creator God, but also Marxists, who insist that the worldwide spread of communism is historically certain.

The title of Jacques Monod's book is a quotation from something that our old friend Democritus said, 2,400 years ago: *Everything existing in the universe is the fruit of chance and of necessity.* So Monod, bringing us up to date, also takes us right back to the start of our story of humanist thinking. But the ideas are no longer mere guesswork: they now have solid scientific facts behind them.

A summary of humanism

Humanism is not a set of doctrines, but an attitude to life. To the humanist, the miracle is here and now. It is the miracle of nature: there is nothing supernatural about it. Because the humanist believes that this life is the only life we can expect to have, it is especially important to make this life a good one. So, although humanism is based on *atheism* or *agnosticism,* it is far more than that negative basis. It also includes positive commitments to make the best possible use of our lives—both for our own sake, and to help others. Humanists are concerned to make the world a better place to live in, not only for people alive today, but for future generations too—especially as the lives of their descendants represent the only sort of immortality that humanists believe in. Above all, humanists regard each individual person as an end in himself or herself; never as a means to achieve something, however desirable the something may be. In order to be a humanist one must be an atheist or agnostic; but it is possible to be an atheist or agnostic without being a humanist. (The Russian dictator, Stalin, was an atheist, but he was certainly not a humanist, because he did not respect the human rights of people who disagreed with him.)

Humanists are also *rationalists*, because they regard human reason as the best guide we have in facing life's problems; but they are more than rationalist, because they take into consideration the whole of human nature (desires, interests, sympathies, imagination, emotions), not just the intellect. In their social outlook, humanists are *secularist,* because they want to free society from the stranglehold that religious beliefs still have on it—whether the morning assembly in British schools or the feeding of sacred cows in Hindu India while human babies starve.

Humanists are *freethinkers,* because they never hand over their minds irrevocably to any Church or Party, but remain free to think for themselves. Humanists use the scientific method, not only to explain nature, but in every aspect of life, and as Bernard Shaw put it, 'never accept anything reverently without asking it a great many very searching questions'. Humanists are *materialists*—having no belief in spirits (mind without body). Humanists are *empiricist* in their approach to knowledge; *utilitarian* in morality; *Epicurean* in the art of living.

Humanists say that every responsible human being should be free to make his or her own choices and live in their own life-style, as long as they do not violate the freedom of others. It would be impossible for humanists to force humanism on other people or persecute nonhumanists, for if they did they would no longer be humanist. Humanism stands for 'the open mind' in 'the open society'. (Athens rather than Sparta.)

Unlike Christians, humanists see no virtue in faith, blind obedience, meekness, unworldliness, chastity, or pointless self-denial. The humanist virtues are: a regard for what is true, personal responsibility, tolerance, considerateness, breadth of sympathy, public spirit, cooperative endeavour, and a concern for the future.

Humanists follow Protagoras and Democritus, not Plato.

3 Reality: true and false

If humanism is a positive outlook in its own right, why do humanists
feel they have to offer reasons for their nonbelief in gods or a future
life? Why use the negative word 'atheist', any more than, say, 'a-fairyist'
or 'a-Santa-Clausist'? (Indeed, some atheists reject the word 'atheist'
because they think it gives the god-idea too much importance.) Why did
Bertrand Russell, in 1927, take time off from his positive contributions
to knowledge to write a popular essay called 'Why I am not a Christian'
for the National Secular Society? And why, in the present book, are the
humanist viewpoint and way of life not simply described, without any
mention of other views?

The answer is that, historically, nonbelievers have been a small
minority in our European culture, and those who think differently
from the majority on any important matter are often expected to
explain why they do not conform to the general opinion. Before long it
will probably be the believers in God and heaven who find themselves
in the position of being asked to justify their belief. But not yet—not
generally, anyway. Most people in Britain still have at least a vague
belief in a personal deity and a future life, even though only a minority
have a strong enough belief to do much about it. So the atheist is still
expected to justify his atheism.

God and Santa Claus

Adults are not expected to mention that they do not believe in Santa
Claus, let alone explain why. But young children who, because of their
age, are assumed to have this belief, often find themselves in the
position of saying 'I don't believe in him.' Other children of their age
(or even, sometimes, teasing adults) may then challenge them about
their denial of Santa Claus. ('Where do you think all the toys came
from that he left at the bottom of your bed at Christmas?') In the same
way, theists often ask atheists 'How do you think the universe came
about, then, if there was no god to make it?'

Not all theists assume that the existence of matter, forming complex
organisms, demonstrates the existence of a creator—and few modern
theologians would claim this—but most ordinary simple people still

22

think so, as St Paul did nineteen centuries ago: 'For the invisible things of him, from the creation of the world are clearly seen' (Romans I). This way of thinking is called 'natural theology'.

Just as very young children think that Santa Claus is a sufficient and necessary explanation for the toys, so unsophisticated god-believers think that a personal creator is a sufficient and necessary explanation for the universe. But as children begin to grow up, they come to realize that the Santa Claus theory raises more difficult problems than the one it purports to solve. And so does the creation theory, though most people never really subject it to critical thought. If they did, they would realize that the idea of a supreme intelligence (without a brain), existing for all eternity, suddenly creating everything else out of nothing, and then keeping a fatherly interest in it all (or at least in one particular little planet), is on the same childish level as the idea of Santa Claus making and distributing all the Christmas toys.

But this analogy holds good only so far. Someone does act as Santa Claus and bring the toys and it is reasonable to seek explanations for such happenings. What we mean by explanations, though, is finding causal relationships between one event and another. When considering the whole universe, as a totality and throughout eternity, it is meaningless to ask for an explanation since there is (by definition) nothing else to relate it to. So god-believers place God outside the universe, as its explanation. But then—what explains God?

Existence

God, it is said, is the answer to the question 'Why does anything exist at all?' But if it is necessary to explain existence, you would still have to explain why and how God existed. So the god-idea doesn't provide a final answer, unless you then assert that God existed from all eternity, uncaused. And why should that be any easier to accept than that matter/energy existed from all eternity, uncaused?

Existence seems such a miraculous thing, it is little wonder that there have been supernatural ideas to account for it from the time that human beings first became capable of abstract thought, nor that such ideas are still widely accepted. But is it reasonable to look for an explanation of existence? There are only two possibilities—either something existing or nothing existing—and the plain fact is that things do exist. You cannot go further back than existence, for there is no prior context of nonexistence in which to place it.

However, it certainly *seems* amazing to us, who are part of it and conscious of it. The mind-boggling vastness of the universe (in relation to human size), its timescale, and its incomprehensible complexity, all add to the wonder of it—though the complexity is possible just *because* of the vastness and the timescale.

For the past four centuries scientists have been discovering how facets of the universe work and how organisms evolve, and, as new evidence emerges, theories previously held become untenable, and new models are proposed that fit the facts better. The whole joy of science is that it is not just a once-for-all revelation but a cumulative human endeavour, continually answering further questions posed by past research. The science of cosmology, especially, is at present in a stage of rapid development, and we are tentatively piecing together the cosmic jigsaw puzzle. Recent discoveries favour the 'big bang' theory for the origin of our universe. But that does not mean it came out of nothing. More likely, the universe 'oscillates' — expanding and collapsing alternately, without any beginning, without any end.

Imagine all the matter of the universe being squashed together to form a very dense mass, so dense that even its light and other forms of radiation are drawn into it But there is a point of density beyond which it cannot go. When that point of contraction is reached, the dense mass explodes into a fireball. Bits fly off like sparks flying. Each 'spark' gives rise to a cluster of galaxies. There are thousands of millions of galaxies, each containing thousands of millions of stars, forming and disintegrating in the process of galactic evolution. Some of the stars have planets associated with them and some of the planets have associated moons. But the galaxies themselves go on rushing away from

The Great Spiral Nebula in
Andromeda, which can
hardly be seen at all with
the naked eye

each other, impelled by the force of that primordial explosion. For thousands of millions of years they go on rushing further and further apart. At some point during galactic evolution, a planet here and there happens to have just the right physical conditions to produce living things, and some of the living things eventually evolve consciousness.

The universe is likely to go on expanding for many millions of years yet, but there is some evidence that the rate of expansion may now be slowing down. This means we can expect the whole process eventually to go into reverse. The universe will begin to collapse, as a ball that has been thrown into the air will reach the height determined by the force with which it was thrown and then succumb to the gravity of the earth. Everything in the universe will then rush together, faster and faster, to form the densest possible mass once more.

Infinity

There is no reason to suppose that this 'oscillating' process ever had a beginning, nor that it will ever end. Indeed, it is far easier to accept as probable the eternity of ever-changing matter/energy (as Democritus suggested nearly five hundred years before the Christian era), than the alternative theory that matter suddenly came into existence at some point in time, before which there was nothing—or nothing except an all-powerful spirit with a creative urge.

The hypothesis of an oscillating universe, for which there is a fair amount of evidence, is surely far more satisfying than belief in a sort of divine conjuring trick, for which there is no evidence whatsoever. Yet many religious people say just the opposite: they say that taking a scientific view of the universe must destroy our sense of awe and wonder, which they often call 'the religious emotion'. But this emotion, which is certainly not dependent upon religious beliefs, comes from thinking about the observable universe. To suggest that trying to understand things scientifically might undermine the magic is like warning people against studying the techniques of Beethoven and Rembrandt lest seeing how they achieved their effects should destroy one's appreciation of their genius. Surely the contrary is the case.

If we contemplate the oscillating universe of eternal units of matter/ energy, all sorts of questions about infinity come to mind. For instance, has a class of pupils identical with those in your classroom today read a book identical with this one, on an identical planet to ours, also called 'Earth', in some former expansion of the universe? And, if so, has it been repeated an infinite number of times? My own conclusion about this is that there may well have been many planets very similar to our

'Reality is the mystery' was the title of the talk being given here by George Melly (jazz singer, musician, film critic, and President of the British Humanist Association) at a meeting of the Central London Humanist Group in 1972

own, with human-like beings educating their children in classrooms with books; and, indeed, there might well be some at the present time in distant parts of the universe, let alone in former universes; but the whole pattern would never be exactly repeated, and no two classrooms would be identical in every respect, since many chance factors, especially of individual heredity, have an infinite range of possible permutations—and one infinity cancels out the other. But it is fascinating to think about—provided you stop when you begin to feel dizzy!

Most educated people today, including theologians, agree with the scientific humanist view that matter/energy has always existed and that life came about through chemical reactions and evolved through mutation and natural selection. Modern theologians often protest when arguments like the above are put, knocking down natural theology—because, they say, Christian faith does not depend on natural theology. This may well be true of their own individual faith, but it is not true of the faith of most Christians. Schoolchildren are still taught natural theology at school; their teachers probably accept it; and so do many clergymen. Even those clergymen who have discarded natural theology for themselves continue to encourage the belief in their congregations—or, at least, say nothing openly to discourage it. But in their scholarly books and lectures theologians say that people need a religious faith not in order to provide supernatural explanations for the natural world but in order to give meaning to their lives.

The argument seems to be that human beings need a superhuman being to look up to, and a life beyond death to look forward to. Whether these are human needs or not, the question still remains as to whether they are actually *true*. But in any case, would a person's life really have no value or purpose unless it were immortal? As Bertrand Russell said, 'Happiness is none the less true happiness because it must come to an end, nor do thought and love lose their value because they are not everlasting.'

Humanists do not believe in cosmic values or ultimate purpose, but they do believe in earthly values and in the individual purposes which we give our own lives as we live them. After all, people go on holiday, even though they know it is just for a week or two. They don't say 'We'll only have to come home again at the end of the holiday, so there is no point in going'. In the same way, life can be worthwhile even though transitory.

Maybe it *would* help to make our lives more satisfactory if there really were an almighty God taking a personal interest in us and we really were going to live for ever in a perfect world. But humanists prefer not to kid themselves with 'wishful thinking'. Admittedly, it often takes courage to face reality and live without the drug of religious belief, but humanists try to cultivate that courage in themselves. They accept life on its own terms—with all its troubles and uncertainties, and with its one final certainty of death—while doing their best to make things better. For it is all the more pressing to do something about unhappiness here and now if you do not believe in a loving god who will see to it that everything turns out right in the end.

Death
Death is generally regarded as an evil—even by people who believe in heaven. But death is essential to life. Without death there could be no birth, no evolution, no younger generations coming along, and certainly no chance of promotion! 'We should not,' said Herbert Samuel, 'see death as an injury, but rather life as a privilege.'

To the humanist, death is simply, as Epicurus said, the end of life. To most religious people, however, it is a transition to a better life. Indeed, it is fair to say that the doctrine of a life hereafter is the one ingredient that makes religion so popular. But this is what Bernard Shaw said about it: 'Now the man who has come to believe that there is no such thing as death, the change so called being merely the transition to an exquisitely happy and utterly careless life, has not overcome the fear of death at all: on the contrary, it has overcome him so completely that he refuses to die on any terms whatever.'

Why are most people so desirous of an afterlife? They generally think of it as life in a perfect world. But a perfect world would necessarily be static—and, surely, very boring!

The chief motive for belief in an afterlife is the unhappiness of being separated from those who are dear to us, particularly when the separation is the permanent one of death. But friends who meet in this life after a lapse of, say, twenty years find that they no longer really know one another. Besides, living on hope is not really living; it is only marking time. To live, you have to build new personal relationships. And even if the belief in reunion gives people comfort, this is no guarantee of its truth.

It is also argued that, since life on earth is so unjust, there must be another life to redress the balance. But why should injustice here lead to an expectation of justice somewhere else?

I have noticed that whenever I question the existence of God, one reply I get is that this world is so wonderful it must have been designed by a supreme being; but when I question the belief in an afterlife, this world is said to be so bad that there must be another one ready to put it right!

The chief *theological* argument for an afterlife is that the existence of an omnipotent God of love demands it. But this world, on the religious theory, is as much God's design as any other, and if he cannot or will not prevent evil from triumphing here, why assume he can or will manage things better elsewhere? Anyway, the argument is pointless except for those who already have an unshakable belief in a God of love and justice.

But is personal survival after death a *possibility*? This raises the whole question of personal identity. What could survive that would still really be *you*? Your identity depends on your memories, your likes and dislikes, and all your funny little ways. These depend on a living brain, on your particular biochemistry, where you live, the way in which you have been educated, and the way life treats you. And, of course,

28

your personality, your opinions, your appearance, and your body cells all change very much during life. Supposing you were to go to heaven exactly as you were the day you were born, or as you may become by the end of a long life, would you regard that newborn baby or that senile centenarian as being really *you?* If you decide that it is the genetic potential that is the real you, what about identical twins? Are they really only one person? The more you think about it, the more snags you will see.

Religious experience

Some of the psychic conditions called 'religious experiences' are fairly common, and very real to the people they happen to. They are sometimes triggered off by religious meditation, but may also be caused by certain drugs, or by music, or by nothing obvious at all. They are a form of ecstasy, and are probably related to sexual emotion. The feeling is sometimes described as one of being absorbed into the cosmos. A single experience can have a lifelong effect on the person's behaviour, especially if he or she believes that it had a supernatural origin. Sudden conversions are often of this nature—but the conversions are to various faiths, so can hardly indicate reliable divine communication.

Human beings have latent mental powers of which they are largely unaware, and this can explain cases of faith-healing and other strange phenomena. But most of the so-called psychic phenomena turn out on investigation to be conjuring tricks, or hallucination, or coincidence, or misremembering, or lies.

But people *want* to believe in such phenomena—particularly ghosts — so that they can contact their dead friends and relations, and as evidence that they themselves will not really die. They want to believe in heaven. They want to believe in an all-powerful God who loves them and will look after them. And so they believe. Some subscribe to incompatible sets of belief at the same time—for instance, Christianity and astrology.

If they derive comfort from their beliefs, is it not wrong to disturb their faith? It would certainly be wrong to take away the religious consolation of anyone who was bereaved or ill or old or dying. But people in normal health are a different matter. Besides, humanists don't force their opinions on other people, as some religionists do; they just say what they really think when the occasion arises. But they do think it important to uphold the truth rather than just what is comforting or advantageous.

Anyway, religious beliefs are by no means always a comfort. They *can* be frightening. And even comfort may not always be a good thing: Karl Marx called religion 'the opium of the people' because it made them content with their lot instead of demanding better conditions. That is why the ruling class has always been in favour of religion. And why, even today, the churches don't have to pay rates and taxes like other organizations. And one reason why there is so much religion in schools and on the radio and television.

Religion in schools
Humanists think it is wrong to indoctrinate children in a particular set of beliefs, especially in a country where beliefs differ as much as they do in Britain today.

In some countries, such as the USA, it is against the law to introduce religion into schools, but in Britain it is actually against the law *not* to introduce it! Under the 1944 Education Act, every school is bound to provide religious instruction and to hold a daily collective act of worship—as though the Parliament of 1944 could guarantee the existence of something or someone that should be worshipped. The law allows parents to withdraw their children from assembly and RE lessons, but most parents are naturally reluctant to make their children feel out of the ordinary. Besides, they might miss some of the announcements made at assembly. And older children who do not believe in God still have to take part in the worship unless they can persuade their parents to withdraw them. Humanists think it should require a positive decision to join an act of religious worship, not someone else's signature to release you from it—an 'opting in', not 'opting out'.

Many teachers who take assembly and RE are not really believers themselves, and sometimes they feel coerced into hypocrisy. Needless to say, this worries religious people as well as humanists. But so far they have been unsuccessful in getting the law changed.

One argument put forward in favour of keeping religion in schools is that without first-hand experience of religion you cannot understand what it means. But, as one who loathed team-games at school, I got some understanding of the joy that ball-game players can experience, not by my own forced participation but by seeing others enjoy themselves in this way—seeing the excitement in their faces and hearing their breathless shouts. So why not just show children films of religious practices, without expecting them to take part in them?

Some Christians have suggested, half-jokingly, that humanists ought

"By the way, Grindley, I take it you're aware of your right to opt out of the daily act of worship?"

A cartoon from *Punch*, showing an unlikely school assembly situation

to be glad that so many children are put off religion altogether by having it drummed into them at school. But humanists are *not* glad about it. Not only does it waste school-time that could be devoted to more worthwhile pursuits; it also has an antieducational effect, so that when children realize that they are being presented with questionable ideas as though they were as uncontroversial as the shape of Australia or an arithmetic answer, there is a danger of their becoming cynical about all the other things they are taught as well. What is more, because morality is falsely associated with religion, they may even start behaving badly when they give up religion.

So humanists are always campaigning for the religious clauses of the Education Act to be repealed. Religious instruction, they say, should be left to the home and the church. They are agreeable, of course, to children learning in school *about* various religions (not just one), together with the religious legends, provided these are presented *as* legends. Also (and far more important) to their being given moral teaching that does not tie morality up with religious beliefs. Humanists would not want children to be taught even humanist ideas alone, as though they were held by everyone.

Humanists are also strongly opposed to denominational (church) schools, because they think every child has a basic right to be part of

31

the common community and meet with ideas at variance with those of the home.

Religious broadcasting

Humanists in Britain complain about the unfair amount of time that is given to Christianity on radio and television—out of all proportion to the number of committed Christians in the country. It is as though almost all the sports time were devoted to one particular sport!

The humanist viewpoint rarely gets a hearing, except as part of a religious discussion, to liven it up a bit—and you always know there will be a Christian spokesman standing by to have the last word.

What humanists would like is for every responsible viewpoint on every subject of social controversy to have its fair say, so that everyone can have access to the knowledge necessary to make up their own minds. The pursuit of truth through a free exchange of views is the most important feature of the ideal known as 'the open society'. We can no longer all meet together, as the citizens of ancient Athens did, so radio and television are vital media of communication.

Is humanism a faith?

Humanists do not have mystic faith, in the sense of believing things on insufficient evidence, but they certainly have faith in human potential.

Because they believe this life is the only life they will have, it is all the more important to humanists to live it to the full, and to provide the best possible conditions of life for people the world over. They put people first. That is what the word 'humanism' means. And they put other animals—not possessions—second, for the animals share our faculty of feeling and suffering.

Because they believe there is no God to turn to, no power to rely on except human powers, humanists stress the importance of self-reliance, human cooperation, and plans based on scientific knowledge. Unlike religious people, who may make some of their decisions according to what the Bible says (or the Qur'an, or other sacred writings) or what their Church teaches, humanists can only rely, in the last resort, on their own judgment based on probabilities indicated by the scientific method.

To those who are used to being offered the ready-cooked meals of religious faith, humanism may seem to offer nothing at all. But it points to the ingredients for making your own meal to your own taste, whether alone or in company with others; and it helps clear a space for you to cook it in.

32

4 Values: good and bad

'What I cannot understand about you humanists,' a clergyman said to me one day, 'is how you can go through life refusing to believe in the existence of good and evil.' 'We believe, of course, in better and worse,' I replied, 'but I suppose you mean God and the devil: absolute good, and absolute evil.' 'You cannot have comparatives without absolutes' was his parting shot. In nature, however, everything is relative; there are no absolutes. Ten inches is longer than nine inches—but is there an absolute longest?

What is conscience?
The idea of absolute perfection, against which everything else must be measured, is part and parcel of the whole religious concept of some other reality behind the reality we experience—a concept which Christianity took over from Platonic philosophy. According to this idea, all the goodness, beauty and truth in this world are reflections of Goodness, Beauty and Truth (the magic of capital letters!) in another, ideal world, which Christians call heaven, and whence, they say, all human values derive. Humanism, on the other hand, recognizes no values for human beings to live by that are not derived from human experience.

But we are left with the philosophical problem of how we judge that one thing is better than another. Is it no more than a matter of taste? Bertrand Russell, after a lifetime immersed in philosophy, was still, in his late eighties, looking for a solution to this problem: 'I find myself incapable of believing,' he said, 'that all that is wrong with wanton cruelty is that I don't like it.' However, philosophers (even humanist philosophers) tend to make extraordinarily heavy weather of quite simple matters. To most of us it is self-evident that it is better for sentient beings to experience pleasure and happiness than pain and misery, and that kindness is therefore good and cruelty is bad. If the philosophers persist in asking *how* we know that pleasure and happiness are better than pain and misery, we can only answer that we know it in our bones. Biologically, the desire to avoid pain and misery evolved as important survival factors, and we are the product of our evolutionary past. The animal desire inbred in us to avoid pain and misery, and to help our own kind to avoid them, reach a high point in human sensibility, and it is this sensibility that gives us our moral and aesthetic values.

For an objective theory of ethics you should look to psychology and sociology rather than abstract philosophy, and see how the human being develops a sensibility and conscience through the social conditioning of early childhood. Small children are very selfish. Then they go through a legalistic, authoritarian stage. Finally, if they come from a loving home, they achieve moral maturity, with a moral code that is utilitarian and reciprocal. If they offend against their own moral code, they feel uncomfortable. And that is what is meant by 'conscience'. There is nothing mystic about it.

Human values

Some religionists protest that this natural explanation dodges the philosophical difficulty, and that belief in God provides external justification for moral (and other) values. But in fact their philosophical argument just goes round and round, like a dog chasing its tail. We know what we ought to do, they say, by finding out what God commands us to do, for whatever God commands must be right. But to say that God's commands are always right requires some way of judging their rightness apart from the mere fact that God commands them; to say that God is good requires some criterion of goodness apart from the statement that goodness comes from God. Otherwise such statements are meaningless. And this brings the argument back where it started: what criteria can there be other than human values? And what is the basis of those values?

Besides, unless we submit God's alleged commands to some sort of human evaluation, how can we be sure that they are in the final interest of human beings? Might not the supposed god be using his human creatures rather as a vivisectionist uses the animals in his laboratory? If such animals were able to understand their situation, they would surely be justified in hating the vivisectionist; and if they had the power to thwart his intentions, they would surely have every right to do so. But in fact such a god would not even have the excuse of the vivisectionist, who at least thinks he is acting for the good of human beings, whereas a divine tormentor could have no motive apart from sadism.

There is also a practical difficulty in the assertion that in order to know what is right we must find out what God commands—the practical difficulty of recognizing the genuine messengers of the divine will, when there are so many rival claimants to the true revelation.

All in all, human reason (fallible though it is), if inspired by human sensibility (however corruptible it may be), is a more reliable moral guide than religious dogma.

The problem of evil

Life is a mixture of good and bad, distributed most unfairly. Some people have more of the good and some have more of the bad—and, of course, this unfairness is something that all decent people deplore and try to do something about. Christians have the consolation of believing that all the injustice in this life will be put right in the next, but humanists, of course, have no such consolation. All they can do is insist on the responsibility of the more fortunate people to help the less fortunate. (That is what humanism is mainly about—but it belongs to the next two chapters rather than this one.)

Since the humanist sees good or bad fortune largely as a matter of impersonal chance, he has no philosophical problem of evil to contend with—only practical problems of how to minimize disease and other evils.

However, to the believer in a personal creator who is both beneficent and all-powerful, evil and misfortune represent a very obstinate philosophical problem. There are several Christian answers to it; they are mostly incompatible, and none of them really provides a solution.

Nature and art

For all its terrible cruelty, nature appeals strongly to the human sense of beauty, and humanists especially turn to nature and art for the sort of satisfaction that religious people can find also in religion. It was a humanist poet, W.S. Landor, who wrote the famous lines

Nature I loved and, next to Nature, Art;
I warmed both hands before the fire of life;
It sinks, and I am ready to depart.

It is a mistake to think that when we say humanism is based on the scientific method this means that the humanist has no use for music, the visual arts, literature, and the beauties of nature. Indeed, his full-blooded and whole-hearted acceptance of the world makes him all the more appreciative of beauty, which is one of the most important factors that make our lives worth living. And maybe the sad fact that nothing of beauty can last for ever makes beautiful things seem all the more beautiful.

In the nineteenth century, when most respectable people in this country still went to church twice on Sundays, the secular societies and ethical societies (which were the forerunners of the humanist groups of today) began to provide for their members the alternative of Sunday evening concerts of secular music—a very daring thing to do in those days. The South Place Ethical Society, which now owns Conway Hall in London, began a series of Sunday evening concerts of chamber-music in 1887, and the series is still going strong today- the 2000th concert in the series having taken place in March 1969. Said to be the longest series of concerts anywhere in the world, it provides music of the highest standard at very low prices.

Late comers.

A printed drawing from the 1890s of South Place concert-goers of the day—the original title rebuking them for their late arrival!

Some people say that since the greatest music ever written was church music and the greatest works of painting and sculpture were of religious subjects, the most potent inspiration of the arts must be religion. But this is not so. Unlike that of the ancient Greeks and the Arabs, the music of the Christian Middle Ages was very inferior, and it was not until the eighteenth century that its great modern development began. Then much of the best church music was composed by men who were apostates from Christianity to humanism. Beethoven, for instance, rejected religion, though he wrote some of the greatest religious compositions of all time. (When a friend jestingly wrote on one of his manuscripts the words 'With God's help', Beethoven altered it to 'Man, help thyself'.) But the Church was the richest employer of musicians and artists for hundreds of years, so the musicians composed masses and the artists painted religious pictures in order to earn a living. Their secular works, however, were of the same high quality.

The wealth of the Church was even more exclusive in the sphere of architecture, as the sublime cathedrals of the Middle Ages bear witness. (Unfortunately, most modern church buildings are far less beautiful!) Ironically enough, humanists are usually among the most ardent preservationists of beautiful churches, though they have no say in the use to which they are put, in spite of the fact that their ancestors, like everyone else's, had to pay (through compulsory tithes, etc) for them to be built. But they regard them as part of our great human heritage of man-made beauty. Just as one can feel reverent awe in the Parthenon without believing in the Greek goddess Athene in whose honour it was built, so one can have similar feelings in Canterbury Cathedral or York Minster without believing in God or Jesus Christ.

As for the beauties of nature, you certainly don't need me to say what delight you can get from a range of mountains or a butterfly wing. But I will close this chapter with a few words from another humanist writer, Llewelyn Powys, who, though a chronic invalid, found great joy in life and nature. *'Oh! how dense we are! The true religion is simple—it is to worship life, beating our foreheads upon the grass in jubilant acquiescence.'*

The Swiss Alps—a scene of natural beauty

5 Morals: right and wrong

The humanist view of morality is that it is simply codes of human conduct, devised by human beings for human benefit.

'It's all very well,' perhaps you are saying, 'but if humanists have no belief in God or a hereafter, why bother to live decent lives? Why not just get whatever they can out of life and let everyone else go hang?'

This line of argument implies that religious people need to be bribed with promises of reward, like naughty children, before they can be expected to behave decently towards their neighbour. But I have a higher opinion than that of people's innate decency—of most people's, anyway. For the fact is that you cannot really enjoy life if you are treating your neighbour in a way that offends your natural human feelings and the social conditioning of your early childhood. Even lower animals (including social insects, such as ants) have cooperative instincts as well as selfish ones, and the survival of a species often depends on a strong cooperative instinct. So it is a part of our evolutionary heritage. In our modern civilization, with news travelling instantaneously around the globe, everybody has become your neighbour; and, unless you are lacking in imagination, you will feel sympathy for people involved in disaster, even in a country you know little about. Doing something to make someone else happier, especially someone close to you but even someone you can only imagine, generally makes you feel happier yourself.

If people really did live good lives only because of the promise of heaven or threat of hell, is that what most of us mean by 'good'? A child might do what it is told in order to get a lollipop, but is it really a good child? If it behaves well in order to be liked by other people, that also is self-interest, but a higher kind of self-interest, independent of the uncertain supply of lollipops.

Free will and determinism

Believers in a good and almighty god generally believe in human freedom of will—for how, otherwise, could human beings be given total blame for their 'sins', let alone for the evils of the world? Most humanists, however, insofar as the old 'free will/determinism' argument lingers on, are determinists. This does not mean that they deny all human freedom and responsibility, but it does mean that we are all less free than we feel we are, since our actions are determined (caused) by the genes we were born with (heredity) and the things that have happened to us in life (environment)—for what else is there to cause them? The interaction of genes and environment determines one's desires, moral fibre, sensitivity, strength of will, intellectual integrity, and so on, and these facets of one's character then become determining factors themselves, affecting one's actions, and being in turn affected by them. So it is well worth cultivating good habits!

Moral rules

There would be no need for any moral rules if you were living alone on a desert island, like Robinson Crusoe. But as soon as Man Friday came along, a reciprocal rule against cannibalism would be necessary if the two inhabitants of the island were to sleep easy.

The moral and legal codes of human communities, such as the Judaeo-Christian Ten Commandments, may contain particular rules that seem a bit pointless, and even religious people sometimes fail to keep the less useful ones ('Remember the Sabbath day to keep it holy') or even the socially important ones ('Thou shalt not steal'). So what about humanists? They do not, of course, subscribe to a written moral code like the Ten Commandments, but they would generally agree with perhaps six of the ten (from number five onwards), subject to reservations for special circumstances.

This broad agreement is no accident, for all moral codes—even those which are said to derive from divine revelation—were designed in the first place for social utility: that is, on the 'utilitarian' principle mentioned in chapter 2. This is not always recognized by later generations trying to live by the moral code, especially if the code is said to be God-given, but those who first laid down the rules (and the supernatural sanctions) were certainly motivated by social (including selfish) utility. The first four of the Ten Commandments were socially useful to those who were trying to weld a number of wandering tribes into a nation, but they are less useful today. That is the worst thing about hard-and-fast rules that are put into sacred books: they cannot be amended to suit changing circumstances. So, although all moral codes begin with a utilitarian basis, religions tend to ossify them, whereas humanism retains the utilitarian principle that keeps the rule relevant.

Utilitarianism

Basically, what the doctrine of utilitarianism says is that the rightness of actions is to be judged by their consequences. This involves a value judgment, and the Utilitarians of the early nineteenth century maintained that what was right was that which promoted 'the greatest happiness of the greatest number'. As a rough guide this is a good principle, but its statistical element might conceivably rob an individual, or a small minority, of the basic conditions necessary to make life worth living at all; and in such a case humanists would put the fundamental happiness of the individual or minority before the superficial happiness of everybody else; for the chief principle of humanism is that every human being is an end in himself or herself, and may never be wholly exploited as a means to an end. It makes sense for those who believe in a life hereafter to sacrifice individual lives, or urge individuals to sacrifice their own lives, in the interests of others, since they believe that the individual will reap a due reward after death; but the humanist has no such justification. The only person who can decide what purposes would be worth sacrificing his life for is, on humanist principles, that person himself.

The golden rule

'Do as you would be done by.' That is good, reciprocal, utilitarian morality. There are two versions of it in the Bible: 'Thou shalt love thy neighbour as thyself', which Jesus quoted from *Leviticus;* and 'Whatsoever ye would that men should do unto you, do ye even so to them.' Other versions of the same advice occur in ancient China (Confucius and Lao-tse), ancient Greece and Rome, and most other civilizations. It is called 'the golden rule'.

But Bernard Shaw wrote: 'Do not do unto others as you would that they should do unto you. Their tastes may not be the same.'

It is clear enough what he was getting at—and *whom* he was getting at: the busybody 'do-gooder' who knows far better than we do what is good for us. Nevertheless, if due allowance is made for differences of taste, the golden rule is an excellent guide in the maze of moral dilemma. And it has its golden feet very firmly on humanist ground, not religious ground—for, whether or not it is given in holy books, it is based on utilitariansim, not on any special revelation, specific commandments, or sacred taboos.

Shaw goes on to say: 'The golden rule is that there are no golden rules.' In other words, there is no rule so golden as to be sacrosanct.

This warning, however, is also very much in the humanist tradition—the tradition of rejecting absolutes, judging every case on its merits, and, above all, treating each individual *as* an individual. Therefore, as Shaw suggests, the rule should be applied with an open

Cartoon of the great freethinker, dramatist and writer, Bernard Shaw (1856-1950), pictured as a rather bad-tempered Santa Claus because he disliked the wastefulness and commercialism of Christmastime

"Courage, friend! We all loathe Christmas; but it comes only once a year and is soon over."

mind and with imaginative respect for minority and personal differences, whether of taste, custom, or sheer cussedness. That said, the golden rule remains the soundest moral principle there is, not only as a guide to individual actions but also as a means of justifying one's actions to others, and, if accepted by them, as an assurance of reciprocity.

It is sometimes suggested that negative versions of the golden rule are more reliable than the positive ones, and perfectly adequate—examples of negative versions being 'What thou thyself hatest do to no man' (*Tobit*) and 'What you would avoid suffering yourself seek not to impose upon others' (the Stoic slave and teacher, Epictetus). And this form of the rule is certainly less vulnerable to Shaw's objection.

Future generations

The golden rule can be applied also towards unborn generations, and, indeed, humanism is deeply concerned with the responsibility of each succeeding generation to bequeath to the future a world as good to live in as possible. After all, while religionists may look to a life hereafter, the only future life for humanists is that of future generations of our species.

It is not surprising, therefore, that humanists are strongly represented in the pressure groups concerned with pollution, conservation, overpopulation, and other aspects of ecology. (For instance, it was a member of the British Humanist Association who started the Conservation Society.)

Since the second world war most educated people have become aware of the threat of ever-increasing human numbers, known as 'the population explosion'—or, rather, it has become too apparent for people to close their eyes to it any longer. The world population explosion started about 1650, and the British population explosion about a hundred years later. The theory of population growth outstripping food supplies was first worked out by an English economist, T.R. Malthus (1766-1834), who advocated cutting down the birthrate by raising the age of marriage!

Towards the end of the nineteenth century, many freethinkers, seeing the need for limiting the population but realizing the impracticality of advocating later marriage, began advocating contraception instead. They were called neo-Malthusians. One of them, Charles Bradlaugh (who was also an important parliamentarian, writer, editor, and reformer, and founder of the National Secular Society) was, in 1877, together with his friend Annie Besant, sentenced to six months' imprisonment plus a £200 fine each (though the convictions were later quashed, on a technicality) for publishing a pamphlet about family planning. People were not allowed to know that it was possible for them to limit their families. They were supposed to leave that decision to God—and then trust in him to provide for their children. Besides, according to the Bible, God had said 'Increase and multiply'. But when that was written, it was necessary to have enough young people coming along to farm the land, and defend it from invasion, and the main danger then was underpopulation, especially in times of plague. But modern medicine changed all that, and the fact that the churches were unprepared to change their teaching to fit in with the changed circumstances, while humanists immediately responded to the new situation, shows that specific commandments are less adaptable than the humanist way of simply putting forward a moral principle on which to base one's decisions.

Sexual morality
Sexual morality is just one facet of general morality, not a special case. Humanists are not among those who condemn all sexual activity outside marriage. Rather, they see sex as one of the great pleasures of life, not just the means of reproduction. But sex is something you have to be even more careful about than crossing the road.

In the sexual field, as in everything else, the general humanist moral principle applies: as long as you are not harming anyone else or imposing your will on anyone else, what you do is your own business.

But it is certainly very immoral to risk conceiving a baby that you do not want and cannot look after, for that possible baby is your responsibility. And there are more than enough babies in the world without having any that are not really wanted, whether inside or outside marriage.

To risk spreading disease from one person to another is also, of course, most immoral. So is playing fast and loose with anyone's affections: you cannot always avoid hurting people's feelings, but you should alway *try* to avoid it. Considerateness (which is application of the golden rule) is one of the most important human qualities, and nowhere more important than in sexual relationships.

What is the humanist attitude to homosexuality? About five in every hundred people are primarily homosexual, yet male homosexuality was against the law until quite recently, and many people were sent to prison for homosexual activity. Humanists, however, regarded it as nobody else's business if two adults of the same sex chose to give each other sexual pleasure. So humanists, in cooperation with some progressive religious people, campaigned for the law against homosexuality to be changed, and eventually it *was* changed in 1967. Since then, homosexual acts between consenting adults have been legal (in England and Wales, though not in Scotland, nor in the armed services or among the crews of merchant ships)—but 'adults' in this law means men over the age of twenty-one, and humanist opinion is that this is too high an age. Most humanists say the age should either be eighteen, since people are now considered adult for all other purposes at eighteen, or else sixteen, since that is the age at which other sexual relationships are allowed by law. So a campaign for the lowering of the age of consent for homosexuals is still going on.

Abortion is another controversial issue. It is a mistake to say that humanists are in favour of abortion: no one can be in favour of abortion, which, except in unforeseen circumstances, is the result of failed contraception. But humanists do regard abortion as better than bringing unwanted babies into the world. In 1936, a group of women, who had been doing pioneering work in the family-planning clinics that were beginning to open in the big towns, set up the Abortion Law Reform Association, because they had seen the terrible results of 'backstreet' abortions to which women resorted for lack of legal abortion. But their Association remained small until 1962, when the thalidomide disaster aroused public demand for abortion to be made legal. Then, with the support of the humanist movement, together with some individuals who were not humanists, the Abortion Law Reform

Association became much stronger and very active, resulting in the passing of the Abortion Act of 1967. This has enabled thousands of women to have abortions carried out properly in hospital, instead of risking dangerous amateur abortions or having babies to whom they could not give proper care. But the chances of getting a legal abortion still depend on the personal views of one's doctor, so the campaign now is for abortion *on request*, as well as having to fight those who want to make abortion illegal again.

Marriage and divorce

Most young adults choose to set up house with one other person of the opposite sex. This is also a very convenient way of bringing up any children they may have. It is usual for the couple to get married—marriage being a social contract to give the partnership stability, mutual insurance, economic security, and recognition by society. But there are some disadvantages in marriage, especially if the partners ever want to dissolve the partnership.

Until 1971, divorce was allowed under English law if only one of the partners wanted it, but not if they agreed about it! Many people, including all humanists, thought this the very opposite of commonsense, so the Divorce Reform Act 1969 was passed, and the courts now recognize one reason only for granting divorce: the irreparable breakdown of the marriage.

Most humanists who want to start a family get married, but some prefer to trust each other without legal marriage. It has even been suggested that living together and having children without the bondage of marriage makes for a stronger bond, and if one or both of the partners want to make love with some new partner there is less pressure to break the first partnership in order to do so.

Those humanists who choose to get married almost always have a registry-office wedding. But those who are members of the South Place Ethical Society (London) can have a special humanist wedding ceremony at the Conway Hall Humanist Centre, which is officially registered (like a church) for weddings. Some humanists think there should be more humanist ritual of this kind, but most think that it is more important to try to get the public facilities improved for the benefit of everybody, whether they are humanists or not—for instance, to get larger and more elegant registry offices for weddings, and to make them available on Saturday afternoons, a popular time for weddings but a time at which one can only get married in church—or in Conway Hall.

A humanist wedding at Conway Hall, London

Freedom to die

Although life is something to be highly prized, certain unbearable conditions—for instance, an incurable disease of a distressing nature—may wipe out all its value. Unlike religious people, most of whom say that the time of death must always be left to God, humanists say there is no purpose in prolonging life beyond the point where it has no more value to the person himself. The humanist sees it as a fundamental human right to be able to choose to die.

Here again it is only comparatively recently that the law of this country has been reformed so as to allow suicide. Until 1961 suicide was illegal—though, of course, it was only *unsuccessful* suicide attempts that offenders could be punished for! (Except, that is, for the 'punishment' of not being given a Christian funeral.)

It is still against the law to help someone else to commit suicide—and, indeed, it is obvious why this should be so. However, humanists think that one kind of suicide help should be allowed—and that is the kind known as 'euthanasia' (easy death), in the case of incurable illness. (Incurable, that is, at the time of decision, and unlikely to become curable during the expected course of the disease.)

Most humanists support the Voluntary Euthanasia Society, which advocates the legalization of a procedure by which healthy adults could sign a document to say that if they should fall victim to incurable illness or injury of a serious and distressing nature they wish to be given a lethal injection. It would then be up to the doctors in charge of the

45

case to decide when that point had been reached, though the consent of the patient would probably be required again, together with that of close relatives and two doctors. But there is a great deal of opposition to this proposal, even though it would affect only those people who were in favour of it.

Another type of euthanasia which some humanists would like made legal is euthanasia for seriously defective newborn babies—and this, of course, could not be voluntary. People who are opposed to it say (if they believe in God) that only God has the right to decide whether a baby, however seriously handicapped, should live or die, and also (whether they believe in God or not) that no one has the right to take any human life but their own, except at that person's free request. People on the other side of the argument say that no one has the right to condemn someone else to *live* when the chances of a worthwhile life are so low. Also, in most cases the parents could produce a perfectly healthy baby in a year's time, and since we now have a social duty to limit our families it is only sensible to limit them to those that have a reasonable chance of a happy life. Besides, at the moment of birth a baby is really only a *potential* human being, for one becomes fully human only through relating to other people. Once a baby gets to know its mother, and the family get to know the baby, it becomes a person, and then it is too late to make such a decision.

Freedom of choice
Adults have a duty to protect the young from doing harm to themselves before they are old enough to understand the consequences of their actions—to protect toddlers from walking into the fire; six year olds from crossing a busy road; twelve year olds from starting the smoking habit; and fifteen year olds from conceiving babies or contracting venereal disease. But once you become adult you become a member of the responsible generation, and humanists do not believe that anyone has the right to take that responsibility from you. Every adult human being of sound mind should have, in the words of John Stuart Mill, 'perfect freedom, legal and social, to do the action and stand the consequences'—provided, of course, one is not thereby infringing the freedom of others. Only by freely choosing what to make of our lives can we attain our full stature and human dignity.

Humanists, therefore, do not agree with censorship, at least for adults. By what right can anyone presume to decide what other people shall be allowed to read? Every member of the responsible generation has the right to choose such things for himself or herself.

John Stuart Mill (1806-1873), a leading Victorian logician, political economist, and feminist, and author of books on *Liberty* and *Utilitarianism*. Gladstone called him 'the Saint of Rationalism'

This does not mean that humanists approve of everything that is printed or filmed or shown on the stage or television, but they say it is up to each individual to decide what he or she shall read or see. At the same time, they uphold your freedom not to have things thrust upon you that you might want to avoid, so items that might offend some people ought to be kept out of public sight, as long as they are freely obtainable by anyone who asks for them, and as long as it is generally known that they are obtainable.

Not only is censorship unjustifiable in itself, but once it creeps in it begins to slow down cultural progress, for things that are considered to be in bad taste often include new ideas of real value.

It is most important that the general public should have all possible information relevant to making up their minds how to act. But if plenty of warning has been given about, say, the grave health risk in heavy smoking, and people still choose to take that risk, then, on humanist principles, no one has a right to stop them from doing so, though one certainly has the right to try to dissuade them.

On the other hand, it is not really fair that people should be tempted by clever advertisements to do things (such as smoking) that are against their long-term interests. So there is a case for curbing such advertisements, which are thrust upon the public unasked for, with the object of making more money for shareholders, even at the risk of causing illness and early death. One of the most useful things you can learn in the modern world is to be wary of the temptations of advertisers. And you should realize how foolish it is to take any drugs just for 'kicks' or to look big, whether drugs that are illegal, such as 'pot' at present, or those that happen to be legal, such as ordinary cigarettes and alcohol. As for 'hard' drugs, which are physically addictive, to have a go at these is really asking for serious trouble that could ruin the whole chance of a full, happy, exciting life, that you won in that cosmic lottery.

6   Living as a humanist

The fact that so far this book has dealt mainly with abstract ideas may have given you the impression that humanism is only for intellectuals. If so, it is a false impression. After all, you would get a similar impression about Christianity from reading a work of theology. And humanism is for living. In fact, living is what it is all about.

Sometimes, when people hear about humanism for the first time, they say 'Well, I've been a humanist all my life, and didn't know it!' And a schoolgirl once asked me 'Why do they have to call it an "-ism"? It's just plain common sense!' But, of course, not everyone agrees with it; though even the traditional religions are becoming more and more humanistic year by year.

Organized humanism

Because humanism has an independent sort of outlook, most humanists see no reason to join a humanist organization. This has the unfortunate result that the membership of the various humanist organizations is only a fraction of the numerical strength of humanism in the population at large, and some people measure its right to have a say in affairs by the number of paid-up members the organizations have, instead of by the number of people who agree with them.

But some humanists do realize the importance of banding together, in order to establish the legitimacy of their views, so that they can profess them with confidence and without injury to their children; also in order to be able to help each other make decisions, for the personal responsibility that humanism entails is too difficult for some people to cope with on their own and it eases the burden to work things out with others who share one's basic assumptions.

In Britain there are three national humanist organizations (British Humanist Association, National Secular Society, and Rationalist Press Association); another which, though not strictly humanist, is essentially humanist in outlook (the Progressive League); a London-based humanist society (South Place Ethical Society) owning the Conway Hall Humanist Centre; and many small local humanist groups. The main reasons for there being so many different bodies are historical; but they each retain their own particular emphasis, though they also work together on particular projects and have a considerable overlap in their membership.

The British Humanist Association (founded 1963) absorbed the Ethical Union (founded 1896). Also from the nineteenth century are the National Secular Society (1866) and Rationalist Press Association (1899). The Progressive League (1932) was founded in response to an idea of H.G. Wells, and had the famous Professor Joad as its first President.

South Place Ethical Society is oldest of all (founded 1793), though it has gone through several changes of name, having evolved from a congregation of Christian dissenters who rejected the prevailing doctrine of hell, through Unitarianism, to a modern humanist position. Among their speakers in the past century are many famous names, including Felix Adler, William Archer, A.J. Ayer, Annie Besant, John Drinkwater, Laurence Housman, Fred Hoyle, Julian Huxley, T.H. Huxley, Cyril Joad, Prince Kropotkin, William Morris, Gilbert Murray, Bertrand Russell, Bernard Shaw, Leslie Stephen, Graham Wallas, Sidney Webb, Rebecca West and Israel Zangwill.

The National Secular Society also has a very interesting history. Its founder, Charles Bradlaugh, was involved not only in the criminal conviction already mentioned, for publishing a pamphlet on family planning, but also in a large number of other court actions, several of which established important principles of civil liberty. In 1880 he was elected as Member of Parliament for Northampton, but his request to substitute secular affirmation for the usual religious oath taken by MPs on entering Parliament was refused, and when he therefore said he would take the oath he was not allowed to do so because of his known atheism, nor allowed to take his seat *without* the oath! So the parliamentary seat to which he had been elected was declared vacant. However, each time a by-election was held in Northampton, Bradlaugh was reelected, and he was finally allowed to enter Parliament in 1886.

Each of the major humanist organizations has a monthly magazine. The Rationalist Press Association publishes *New Humanist;* the British Humanist Association has its *Humanist Newsletter*; the Progressive League, *Plan;* and South Place Ethical Society, *The Ethical Record;* while *The Freethinker* is published in association with the National Secular Society.

The first editor of *The Freethinker,* G.W. Foote (1850-1915), was sent to prison for a year in 1883 for the crime of 'blasphemy'. Bradlaugh tried in vain to get the Blasphemy Laws repealed, and they

Cartoon from a
contemporary magazine
of Charles Bradlaugh
(1833-1891), pictures
him as a stubborn
elephant, difficult to
remove from
Parliament

are actually still on the statute book, though the last time anyone was imprisoned for blasphemy was in 1922, when J.W. Gott was cruelly sentenced to nine months' imprisonment with hard labour, which caused his early death.

In addition to the campaign against the Blasphemy Laws and to all the political and social campaigns mentioned in chapter 5, the humanist movement has fought consistently for women's liberation (since more than a century before 'Women's Lib'), for prison reform, for the abolition of capital punishment (finally achieved in 1965), for the abolition of corporal punishment (still allowed in schools, but much more restricted than it used to be), for the better treatment of the insane, for the abolition of cruel sports, and for innumerable other social causes, as well as such minor freedoms as Sunday entertainment (extended in 1972) and Sunday trading.

Overseas humanist organizations

Most countries have their own humanist organizations, many of them federated through the International Humanist and Ethical Union, which was formed in 1952 and has consultative status at UNESCO. They each apply the general humanist principles to their own situation, and their activities vary according to existing laws and customs. But the direction in which all of them are moving is towards the secularization of society and greater freedom for the individual.

Ceremony

The ritualistic ceremonies provided by some humanist organizations also vary from country to country, according to the expectations of each particular culture. The British do not seem to feel the need for much ritual in their lives, and the only humanist ceremony for which there is much demand in Britain is the funeral. Most humanists are cremated, and all the British national humanist organizations plus some of the local ones will arrange for funeral officiants to take the place of a minister of religion. There is also a (much smaller) demand for humanist weddings, and a very occasional request for a baby-naming ceremony.

In some countries, however, there are many more humanist ceremonies. In Norway, for instance, where it is the custom for almost every adolescent to be confirmed, young people from humanist families would feel they were missing something if they did not have their own growing-up initiation ceremony, so, after receiving a course in moral studies, they take part in a 'civil confirmation' ceremony in their humanist group, as a sign that they have become adult.

Social action

Humanist organizations do not duplicate social work that is being done well by other bodies. And even if it is not being done well but public resources are there for doing it, they prefer to act as a pressure group to get it done better by the proper agency, than to set up a new charity. As individuals, they tend to do voluntary work through the United Nations agencies, national and local welfare services, and undenominational voluntary bodies with specific aims. But where there is a gap, they try to fill it.

For instance, there used to be a gap in the facilities for the adoption of babies, because most adoption societies were run by religious denominations on a religious basis, so that people of no religion found it almost impossible to adopt babies at all. In addition to pressing for nondenominational adoption facilities to be provided by local councils, the national humanist organizations got together in 1963 to found the Agnostics Adoption Society, which later changed its name to the Independent Adoption Society. It is now generally recognized as one of the best-run adoption agencies in the country.

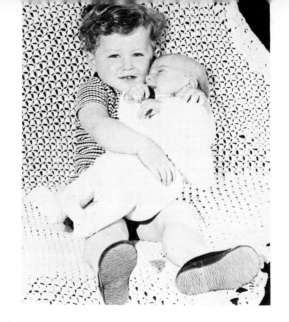

A new brother: two
little boys adopted by
the same family through
the Independent Adoption
Society

At the other end of life, there was another need—elderly people needed homes where they could retain their independence yet have companionship and help when required. So the Humanist Housing Association was formed in 1954 to provide flatlets where elderly people could spend their remaining years in modern comfort, with their own furniture and possessions, looking after themselves, but with a warden on call in case they needed any help, and communal gardens and sitting-rooms for when they wanted company. This has now become a widely accepted pattern for homes for the elderly.

Rose Bush Court, in Parkhill Road, London—one of the blocks of flatlets built by the Humanist Association for elderly people

The Humanist Counselling Service fills another gap, to help and advise people who do not belong to a church and so have no church minister to turn to when they are depressed or in trouble.

Most of the local humanist groups support particular local, national, or international social projects, and a few have set up their own projects for social action. Some, for instance, have formed 'threes' groups of Amnesty International, helping prisoners of conscience and their families. One of the most impressive projects for which a local humanist group has been responsible is the hostel scheme (comprising small, family-sized units) which was founded by Edinburgh Humanist Group for teenage boys with no stable homes.

In Botswana (Africa), a chain of secondary schools, which specialize in teaching agriculture, was started by a few humanists, and British humanists raised the £1,000 necessary to get it started. The actual building work was carried out by the students themselves, who even made the bricks for it!

Another humanist project was set up in a poor district of Bihar (India) to supply such primary needs as wells and irrigation. Money for this project was raised by the International Humanist and Ethical Union from humanists in all their member countries.

Mostly, however, humanists support such organizations as Oxfam, which have more resources for worthwhile schemes.

In any case, the humanist emphasis in social work is not so much to give people things and do things for them, but to help them to help themselves. What people want, the world over, is the opportunity to work for the fulfilment of their own life's purposes, free from oppression and discrimination. And this is what humanism is about.

Students building their own school at Swaneng, Botswana, as part of a project started by humanists, in association with War on Want, and later maintained by the Botswana government

53

Suggestions for further reading

An ordinary encyclopedia will provide articles on most of the '-isms' mentioned in this book. Further information about humanism, including free pamphlets, can be obtained from any of these three organizations:
British Humanist Association, 13 Prince of Wales Terrace,
London W8 5PG
National Secular Society, 698 Holloway Road, London N19
Rationalist Press Association, 88 Islington High Street,
London N1 8EN

They will also supply, as indicated, the following books:

BHA (1970) *Toward an Open Society* Pemberton (BHA, RPA)
BHA Education Committee (1971) *Education for the Open Society*
    British Humanist Association (BHA)
BHA Education Committee (1972) *Honest to Our Children*
    British Humanist Association (BHA)
H.J. Blackham (1968) *Humanism* Penguin (BHA)
Brigid Brophy (1969) *Religious Education in State Schools*
    Fabian Society (BHA, NSS)
J.B.S. Haldane (1968) *Science and Life* Pemberton (BHA, RPA)
Hector Hawton (1971) *Controversy* Pemberton (BHA, NSS, RPA)
Hector Hawton (1963) *Humanist Revolution* Pemberton (BHA, NSS,
    RPA)
James Hemming (1970) *Individual Morality* Panther (BHA)
Julian Huxley (1967) *Religion without Revelation* C.A. Watts (BHA)
Margaret Knight (1961) *Humanist Anthology* Pemberton (BHA, NSS,
    RPA)
Margaret Knight (1955) *Morals without Religion* Dobson (BHA)
Margaret Knight (1974) *Honest to Man* Elek/Pemberton (NSS, RPA)
Kit Mouat (1972) *An Introduction to Secular Humanism* published
    privately (NSS)
Royston Pike (1963) *Pioneers of Social Change* Pemberton
    (BHA, RPA)
Winwood Reade (1968) *Martyrdom of Man* Pemberton (NSS, RPA)
Bertrand Russell (1961) *Let the People Think* Pemberton (RPA)
Bertrand Russell (1957) *Why I am not a Christian* Allen and Unwin
    (NSS)

Acknowledgments

The author and publishers wish to thank the following for their help in providing the photographs and drawings which illustrate this book: Aldus Books Limited, London, pp 6, 10 (taken from *The Growth of Ideas*, diagrams by Ted Powers and Gordon Cramp respectively); Charles Edridge, photographer, pp 26, 52 bottom; Paul Elek Books Limited, London, p 50 (taken from David Tribe *President Charles Bradlaugh, MP*); Mr and Mrs B. Hartnett p 45; Independent Adoption Society p 52 top; Mansell Collection pp 9, 11, 15; Museum of the History of Science, Oxford, p 14; National Portrait Gallery, London, p 47; Paul Popper Limited pp 19, 24, 37; *Punch* p 31; Shaw Society p 41; South Place Ethical Society p 36; Staatliche Museen, Berlin, p 7; Trustees of the British Museum p 17; War on Want p 53.

Index